W is for W

Find the Sup

by Linda Daugherty and Sandra Koch

ISBN – 13: 978-1974269495
ISBN - 10: 1974269493

Printed and bound in the United States.

Wonderkids Photo Credits:

A –Linda Daugherty
B –Linda Daugherty
C –Sandra Koch
D - Sandra Koch
E – David Kaye
F – Sandra Koch
G –Sandra Koch
H –Linda Daugherty
I – Julia Price Mayers
J – Linda Daugherty
K –Linda Daugherty
L – Sandra Koch
M -Amy Aadland
N –Sandra Koch
O –Sandra Koch
P – Sandra Koch
Q –Amy Aadland
R – Sandra Koch
S – Sandra Koch
T – Sandra Koch
U – Christine Wortham
V – Ann Marie Duff
W – Mandy Gates
X – Sandra Koch
Y – Sandra Koch
Z – Jaimee Herrara

Cover photo – Jaimee Herrara

Collage Photos, clockwise – Jaimee Herrara, Sandra Koch, Sandra Koch, Jeffrey Mayers, Linda Daugherty, Jaimee Herrara, Sandra Koch, Sandra Koch

Note to Caring Adults

It is our choices that show what we truly are,
far more than our abilities.
~J.K. Rowling, from *Harry Potter and the Chamber of Secrets*

Character building is one of the most valuable gifts we can give our children. Learning about positive behavior begins at an early age as children move from playing by themselves to playing with others and becoming more aware of the world around them. The research on bullying and the negative effects on society continue to be alarming. *W is for Wonderkid* offers an opportunity to discuss, practice, and model ways children can help build their super powers, and make the world a kinder environment.

The 26 easy-to-memorize, read-aloud rhymes in this book help develop a Wonderkid character-building vocabulary, and skills to use when confronted with bullying. They can be read in order from A to Z, or by a specific letter or concept. The questions and definitions can be used at any time to further discussions with children.

Share your own experiences as well. This encourages further communication, understanding of the concept, and how others handle various life situations, including bullying. Their responses will allow you to find out what the child is thinking and give you a window into their world.

Whether their cape is visible or invisible, all children can be Wonderkids. *W is for Wonderkid* has been created to enhance the growth of all children, and encourage a sense of caring and responsibility. Through this book, the child will develop their powers, and become aware of their actions and how those actions influence others. Watch for character-building moments that occur each day and help children build their Wonderkid skills!

Linda and Sandra

This book is dedicated to all the children and students who have impacted our lives, as well as the caring adults who are helping to make a difference one child at a time.

Thank you to our friends and colleagues, for listening, reading, discussing, and lending us their classrooms to create a tool which was child-centered, and user-friendly.

Most importantly, we thank our families for their never-ending love, as well as their support of our vision.   Their patience with the process has been a priceless gift.

A is for **ACTION**

I can show that I care,
By the way I treat others
Anytime, anywhere.

Actions:
Wonderkids
show caring
with all their
might.

How do you show caring for others?
Does a bully show caring for others?

B is for **BRAVE**

It's not easy you know.
Bravery takes courage
And helps me to grow.

Bravery:
Wonderkids
do something
even if they
are afraid.

What do you do when you are afraid?
What do you do when you are faced with a bully?

C is for **CREATE**

I have a problem, what do I do?
Think of ways to solve it,
There are usually quite a few!

> **Creative:** Wonderkids keep on trying to think of a different idea, or way to solve a problem.

Who do you talk to if you have a problem?
When have you had to solve a problem at home or play or school?

D is for **DECIDE**

What should I say or do?
I try making good choices,
But it's not always easy to.

Decision: The action Wonderkids choose after considering all the options.

How do your choices affect others?

E is for **EMPATHIZE**

I am loving and aware.
We all have feelings to consider,
And it's important to show I care.

> **Empathy:**
> Wonderkids understand that others, including animals, have needs and feelings, too.

How do you treat others?
Why is it important to think about others?

F is for **FORGIVE**

I may be angry for what somebody did,
But I will try to forgive them,
Cause that's being a Wonderkid.

Forgiveness: Wonderkids try not to be mad at someone forever.

When have you been angry at someone?
What did you do about it?

G is for GIVE

I'll show that I care.
Food, toys and love,
Are great things to share.

Giving: Wonderkids make people happy by spending time with them, or sharing, giving or donating to those in need.

How have you shared with others in some way?

H is for HELP

There is always work to be done.
I'll find ways to help others,
Helping can be fun!

Helpful:
Wonderkids
make things
easier for
others.

Who helps you?
Is it okay to ask for help? How do you help others?

I is for **INTEGRITY**

Wonderkids do the right thing,
Even when no one is looking...
And no matter what it brings.

Integrity:
Wonderkids choose to
do the right thing,
no matter the
consequence.

*How do you know if your
choice is the right thing?
What if telling the truth
gets you in trouble?*

J is for **JOY**

I'll choose to smile instead of frown.
When things don't work out right,
I won't let it get me down.

Joyful:
Looking at things with a positive attitude.

Is it okay to be sad or angry?
What do you do when you are sad or angry?
Is it okay to hurt others if you are angry?

K is for **KIND**

I'll find moments each day
To make others feel special
In my own caring way.

Kindness:
Wonderkids are
nice to
everyone.

What do you do that is kind?
What do you do if someone is not kind to you?

L is for **LOYAL**

I'll be a friend who will care.
No matter what happens,
I'll choose to be there.

> **Loyalty:** Wonderkids stay true to others.

What do you do to show you are loyal to someone?
What do you do to show you are loyal to your friends, even if you are mad at them?
What do you do if you see someone bullying your friend?

M is for **MANNERS**

I'll make good choices every day.
I'll be polite to others,
In all I do and say.

Manners:
Wonderkids
demonstrate
choices that
show respect
for others.

What do good manners look like?
Have you ever had to tell someone to "Stop it,"
or "Don't do that again"?

N is for **NAUGHTY**,
And also for **NICE**.
Wonderkids choose what's right,
Without thinking twice.

Naughty: A choice that hurts yourself or others.

Nice: A choice that helps yourself or others.

*Does it make it okay to say, "I am sorry" or
"It was an accident" and then do something naughty again?*

O is for **OBEY**

I will try to follow the rules.
Rules are used to guide me,
At home, at play, at school.

Obedient: Wonderkids follow rules that keep them safe and help them grow.

Why do we need rules? What rules do you have to follow?

P is for **PAUSE**

Before deciding what to do,
I will stop, be still, and think
How my choice affects me and you.

Why is it important to pause?
What could you do when you need to stop and think?

Pause: Wonderkids wait for a moment, and think about what the consequences would be because of their actions.

Q is for **QUIET**

I will slow down the pace.
I'll take time to be still,
I'm not running a race.

Why is it important to take time to be quiet?
What do you do to calm down when you get frustrated or upset?

Quiet:
Wonderkids find ways to be calm, and enjoy peaceful moments each day.

R is for **RESPECT**

We share the earth together.
I value people, places and things,
To make the world even better.

Respectful: Wonderkids are good citizens who show consideration for others, as well as the environment.

How do you show respect wherever you are?

S is for Statements

I will use my words with care.
Words can help or hurt someone.
I will stop and be aware.

Statements:
Statements are words someone says or writes.

What words do you use to tell people how you are feeling?
What words have you heard that helped someone?
What words have you heard that hurt someone?

T is for **TRUST**

Each and every day,
I'll be a person others believe
By the things I do and say.

Trustworthy: Wonderkids keep their word and help others feel safe and secure.

What do you do that shows others you can be

trusted? Why is it important to tell the truth?

U is for **UNDERSTANDING**

Everyone is special in their own way.
Find the good things in others,
Being different is okay!

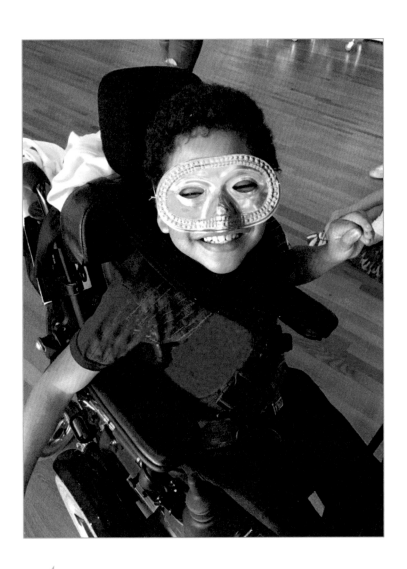

Understand:
Wonderkids
are tolerant
and accepting
of the needs,
feelings, and
views of
others.

What does it mean to be tolerant? How do you show tolerance or understanding of others? How are you different from others?

V is for **VICTORIOUS**

In everything I do,
I'll do the best job I can
'Cause that's what Wonderkids do!

Victory:
Wonderkids are winners because they never stop trying.

What is difficult for you to do? What do you do about it?
Do superheroes give up if something is difficult?

W is for **Wonderkid**

I'll be the best that I can be.
I'll try to make good choices each day,
Which helps both you and me.

Wonderkid: Someone who keeps on trying to do the right thing, and make the best choices they can.

Is it difficult to make the right choices sometimes? If so, what do you do?

X is for **eXtraordinary**

Going above and beyond is rare.
I show I am a Wonderkid when
I work to show I care.

eXtraordinary:
The things
Wonderkids do
to help make
the world a
better place.

What extra things do you do for others?
How do you help make the world a better place?

Y is for **YES!**

I will be a good sport.
I'll celebrate people doing their best,
With smiles, and claps and support.

Yes!:
Wonderkids
celebrate the
accomplishments
of themselves
and others.

How do you act when a team wins, or loses, a game you are playing or watching? How do you act when you win or lose a board game or other activity?

Z is for **ZOOM!**

Put on your cape and fly!
Practice making good choices daily,
Wonderkids reach for the sky!

> **Zooming:**
> Wonderkids zoom in on building their super powers every day.

Does your cape have to be visible for you to be a Wonderkid?

Be a Wonderkid!

Find the Superhero in You

Made in the USA
Lexington, KY
20 August 2017